Elephants

Elephants

by Sarah Albee

Reader's Digest

YOUNG FAMILIES

Published by The Reader's Digest Association Limited

London • New York • Sydney • Montreal

CONTENTS

Chapter 1

An elephant story 6

Chapter 2

The body of an elephant 14

Chapter 3

Meals and baths 26

Chapter 4

Elephant families 32

Chapter 5

Past and future 38

Glossary

Wild words 44

Index 46

An elephant story

Little Elephant looked up. Dark clouds were zooming across the sky. The long, dry season was coming to an end at last. Her mother stood nearby, along with several of Little Elephant's aunts, all of them keeping a close eye on their little ones.

Every day Little Elephant was able to do more for herself. Soon her mother would be ready to have another baby. Little Elephant couldn't wait to have a new brother or sister to play with!

The elephants in the herd stamped and snorted restlessly. Big drops of rain began to fall. Little Elephant's skin shone as she grew wetter. The rain felt wonderful!

For the next week or so, the herd trudged across the wide, open plains. Now that the rainy season had arrived, the elephants were following Big Elephant to the river. She was Little Elephant's great-aunt and the largest elephant in the herd. She had lived a very long time and knew just where to go.

Little Elephant's group arrived at the marshlands near the river, where tender green reeds grew quickly. There was plenty of food and water for everyone. Little Elephant trumpeted happily. She had spotted another group of elephants. They were part of a larger clan that shared a home range with Little Elephant's group.

It was not just by chance that the groups had joined up. Big Elephant had been sending signals to the other group as they crossed the grassy plain, low rumbles that no human could ever hear. The other elephants had signalled back, telling Big Elephant just where they were.

Little Elephant hurried over to greet the young elephants in the group. They twined their trunks around one another, trotted in circles, roared and rumbled. Then Little Elephant and her friends jumped into the muddy water and rolled and splashed. They picked up mud with their trunks and slapped it against their bodies to cool off.

DID YOU KNOW?

Elephants are the second tallest animals in the world. The tallest are giraffes.

Suddenly Big Elephant let out a bellow. All the elephants started to stamp and snort and trumpet with joy. A new baby boy elephant had been born to Little Elephant's mother.

When Big Elephant gave the signal, Little Elephant hurried over to greet her new baby brother. Using her tusks and her trunk, their mother was gently helping him to stand up on his wobbly legs. He was learning to balance himself on his four legs. Little Elephant touched him gently with her trunk. She had so much to teach her little brother about being an elephant.

Furry babies

Baby elephants are born with black fur covering their skin. Most of it falls off. When baby elephants grow up, they will continue to have thick hairs at the end of their tails and a little hair on their faces.

Like lions, bears, rabbits and humans, elephants belong to the group of animals scientists call mammals. And all mammals have hair.

Chapter 2

The body of an elephant

The huge ears of African elephants are the same shape as the continent of Africa!

DID YOU KNOW?

Elephants are the largest land animals in the world.

Two kinds of elephants

Asian elephants

Elephants who live in Asia are smaller than African elephants and have smaller ears. They have two bumps on their foreheads.

There are two kinds of elephants. One lives in Asia. The other lives in Africa. The biggest difference between the two is the size of their ears. Asian elephants have much smaller, more pointed ears. African elephants have huge ears that are rounder in shape and rise above their necks.

Asian elephants are shorter and smaller than their African relatives. Asian elephants are about 2.7 metres tall at the shoulder compared with African elephants, which are 3 to 4 metres tall.

Asian elephants are somewhat different in shape, too. They have more of a dome-shaped head and a rounder body with a humped back. The backs of African elephants have a slight dip in the middle.

All African elephants have tusks. The tusks are very big. In Asia, only male elephants have tusks.

The trunks of African elephants have two 'fingers' at the tip. Asian elephants have only one.

A hunk of a trunk

The trunk of an elephant is amazing. It is strong enough to lift a log that weighs 250 kilos yet dainty enough to pluck a single blade of grass. It can bend, twist, stretch and curl. It can suck up, spray or hold more than 9 litres of water. It is packed with taste and smell sensors – elephants can smell water miles away. The trunk caresses other elephants, perhaps to show affection and tenderness. But the main task of a trunk is to carry food and water to the elephant's mouth.

The trunk is a continuation of the elephant's nose and upper lip. It can be almost 2 metres long and has no bones in it at all. It is made completely of muscle – some scientists think it has more than 40,000 separate muscles!

The trunk of an elephant serves as the animal's hand and nose. It can do many amazing things.

Nose fingers

An African elephant's trunk has two flexible flaps at the tip that work together, somewhat like your thumb and first finger, to pick up small objects. An Asian elephant's trunk has just one flap, which also works like a finger.

Elephants use one tusk more than the other, just as we use one hand more than the other. The main tusk is rounder at the tip from use and sometimes it is shorter than the other tusk.

Giant-size teeth

The tusks of an elephant are as amazing as its trunk. Tusks are giant-size incisor teeth, and they continue to grow throughout the animal's lifetime. The tusks of a male elephant can be more than 3 metres long. The tusks are used for digging, peeling bark from trees, lifting things, and when necessary, as weapons. In Africa all elephants grow tusks. Among Asian elephants, only males develop tusks.

In addition to tusks, elephants have four huge teeth inside their mouths. One tooth can weigh more than 5 kilos. Like your molars, elephant teeth have ridges for grinding up food. When a tooth gets worn out, a new one grows. Elephants grow six sets of teeth in their lifetime. The last set appears when the animal is about 40 years old.

Ivory tusks

Unfortunately for elephants, humans have prized ivory over the centuries. Because elephants are now an endangered species, the business of selling ivory has been banned. Still, illegal ivory hunters exist.

On tiptoe

Elephants are very sure-footed. They step quickly and almost soundlessly, which is surprising in such large animals.

Elephants can walk forwards and backwards. They can run and swim, but they cannot jump.

● Elephants have toes, although we can only see some of the toenails. Elephants walk by putting their toes down first, then the heel. The elephant's weight is supported both by the tip of the toe and a thick, squishy foot pad in the heel that acts as a cushion.

● The foot pad is actually a spongy layer of skin that expands as the foot is placed down. The ridges on the bottom of an elephant's foot grip the ground much the way a person's hiking boots do, allowing the elephant to climb hills and walk on rocks quite easily.

● Elephants can support their weight on their hind legs. This enables them to reach leaves growing high on trees.

Elephants walk several miles in a day and may travel as many as 50. They usually move at about 4 to 5 miles per hour, but they can sprint (for a short distance) at a rate of 30 miles per hour. That's faster than the fastest human sprinters who run short distances at about 20 miles per hour.

The skin of elephants is very thick but also very sensitive. An elephant can feel a fly landing on its skin!

24

Wrinkly skin

Elephant skin is very wrinkly. African elephants have wrinklier skin than their Asian relatives. The wrinkles come in handy. They allow the animal to move about freely, as if dressed in a roomy suit of clothes, to bend and kneel and run. Also, the cracks and grooves in the skin trap water and mud, allowing slow evaporation of water. This helps to keep the elephant cool on hot days. The mud also helps to prevent sunburn.

Another word for an elephant is a pachyderm (pronounced *PACK-ih-derm*). It is the Greek word for 'thick-skinned'. The skin of an elephant can be as much as 6 centimetres thick in some places. But although it is thick, an elephant's skin is very sensitive.

Flapping ear fans

Elephant ears are perfect natural air conditioners. The ears have lots of blood vessels close to the surface of the skin. As air moves over the ears, it cools the blood vessels. Cooler blood then circulates around the elephant's body.

African elephant ears can wave like huge fans, letting body heat escape.

Chapter 3

Meals and baths

Elephants can spend 16 hours a day eating!

DID YOU KNOW?

If an elephant is sick and can't walk to food, other members of the family will bring food to him or her.

What elephants eat

Three meals a day

Although elephants spend most of their time eating, they eat three 'meals' a day just like you – morning, afternoon and night.

At noon, when the sun is hottest, elephants find shade and sometimes doze while standing up. At night, though, they lie down on their side to sleep.

Elephants need to eat enormous amounts of food to support their huge size. A large male can eat more than 200 kilos of food every day! This explains why elephants spend most of their day eating. Elephants are herbivores, which means they eat only plant matter and no meat. In addition to grasses, leaves and fruits, elephants eat twigs and tree bark.

Like other herbivores, elephants crave salt and other minerals that plants do not provide. So elephants eat the soil, because it has the nutrients they need. Like natural bulldozers, elephants dig up the earth with their tusks, grind the soil and rock into powder with their teeth, and swallow.

Hungry elephants in search of food can be very destructive, especially when food is scarce. Elephants will strip shrubs of their leaves and knock down trees to get at the leaves on top. But elephants change the landscape in good ways, too. By eating shrubs and small trees, they thin out thickly wooded areas, letting in sunshine for new plants to grow. And since elephants don't fully digest all that they eat, their dung contains seeds that help to spread new plant life.

Water works

Water is very important to elephants, and they never go very far from it. Elephants need to drink a lot of water to survive. Just one elephant can drink more than 180 litres of water a day! To drink, an elephant draws up water through its trunk and then squirts the water into its mouth. A baby elephant has to kneel down to drink until it learns how to use its trunk.

Elephants love to soak in watering holes. Soaking in deep water lets the elephant take weight off its feet and legs, something which must come as a great relief for an animal that weighs around 6 tonnes!

Elephants also love to swim. They can swim several miles at one time. They may even use their trunks as snorkels.

Sometimes, during periods of drought, water may not be visible, but older elephants are very good at finding it. They loosen the soil with their tusks and use their trunks to dig. And they can dig holes that are more than 2 metres deep! Other animals know that elephants can find hidden water and so they often follow elephants, hoping to benefit from their natural well-digging services.

Elephants love to play in the water and splash and spray for fun – as well as to cool down and to get rid of annoying insects.

DID YOU KNOW?

After bathing, elephants dust themselves with dirt or roll in the mud to coat themselves. The mud keeps the animals cool and their skin soft. It also helps to protect against insects and sunburn. Covered in mud, young elephants have fun slipping and sliding over each other. Sometimes older elephants join in and play, too.

Chapter 4

Elephant families

Keeping in touch

Elephants are very caring animals. If a baby elephant takes a nap, the group will wait until it wakes up before moving on. If a member of the herd is sick or wounded, the other elephants will not leave it.

Elephants live in small family groups of about eight to ten animals, led by a female elephant. Scientists call her the matriarch (pronounced *MAY-tree-ark*). She is usually the oldest animal in the group, often more than 60 years old. As elephants continue to grow throughout their lives, the matriarch is also the herd's largest animal. The matriarch is responsible for the safety of the group and for making sure that all the elephants have enough food and water. When groups of elephants travel or stay together for a time, they are called a herd of elephants.

Elephants keep in contact using sounds. Their usual call is a low rumbling noise. Humans cannot hear it, but other elephants can — from as far as 6 miles away! Elephants also make trumpet calls, roars and screams.

Like people, elephants communicate using body language. When they are relaxed, their trunks hang down and their ears are back. When they are angry, they flare out their ears, pull back their trunks and tuck their heads down with their tusks pointing forward. Elephants warn away intruders by making threatening signals, such as whirling their trunks around, beating them against the ground or tossing up a cloud of dust.

Big babies

When a mother elephant is ready to have a baby, the other elephants in the group gather around to protect her from any predators. One female helps her with the birth. The newborn elephant, called a calf, weighs more than 90 kilos and is about 90 centimetres tall! Within an hour, the calf can stand up on its own. All the elephants welcome the big little one by stamping their feet and making trumpet calls.

The mother elephant is very protective of her baby and rarely lets it out of her sight. For the first few months, the baby elephant lives only on its mother's milk, then adds plant food to its diet. A calf will drink about 30 litres of milk a day until the age of two. By six years of age, Asian elephants can weigh a tonne – 1,000 kilos! Because they drink mother's milk, young elephants can spend a lot of time playing rather than having to search for food. Playing helps them to learn important skills for survival. Calves run around, charge after birds and play-fight.

Like humans, elephants have a long childhood. They learn many skills from the older elephants in their group. Sisters, aunts and grandmothers help the mothers to take care of and teach the young elephants.

A comfort trunk

An elephant calf sucks on its trunk for comfort just as a human baby sucks his or her thumb.

DID YOU KNOW?

Female elephants give birth to just one baby elephant at a time. Scientists call the baby a calf. Female elephants may have four to six calves during their lifetime.

A baby elephant is small enough to walk under its mother's stomach, where it will be very safe. A young calf often wraps its trunk around the mother's tail so that the pair don't get separated from each other.

Chapter 5

Then and now

Big and small relatives

The ancient relatives of elephants belong to a group of animals scientists call Proboscidea (animals with a trunk). Mammoths and mastodons, which became extinct about 10,000 years ago, were members of this group. They were nearly the same size as modern-day elephants but had long, shaggy fur and huge, curled, 5 metre long tusks. Woolly mammoths lived in very cold places.

The closest living relatives of elephants today include hyraxes (furry, rabbit-size mammals) that live in Africa and parts of the Middle East and manatees (sea cows).

FAST FACTS ABOUT ELEPHANTS

SCIENTIFIC NAME	African elephant Asian elephant	*Loxodonta africana* *Elephas maximus*
CLASS	Mammals	
ORDER	Proboscidea (animals with trunks)	
SIZE	African elephant (male) Asian elephant (male)	3 to 4 metres tall 2.7 metres tall
WEIGHT	African elephant (male) Asian elephant (male)	6 tonnes 5 tonnes
LIFE SPAN	Up to 80 years	
HABITAT	African elephant Asian elephant	savannah, forest forest, grassland

Elephants live in a wide range of habitats, from savannahs to forests. When the sun is hottest, they seek whatever shade they can find.

Where elephants live

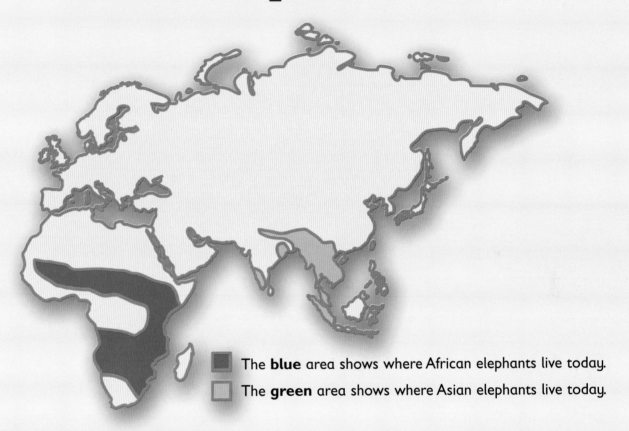

The **blue** area shows where African elephants live today.

The **green** area shows where Asian elephants live today.

Because they are huge, elephants have few natural enemies. Baby elephants may be hunted by lions (in Africa) or tigers (in Asia), but are usually well protected by adult elephants.

The greatest threat is humans. Elephant tusks are made of ivory, which has been highly prized for centuries. To take the tusks, the elephant must be killed. Trading in ivory was banned in 1989, but people still kill elephants and sell ivory illegally.

Elephants used to live all over Africa but now live in only a third of the continent. Here and in Asia, their numbers are falling as more and more of their natural habitat is cleared for building, mining and farming.

GLOSSARY OF wild WORDS

banned	forbidden by law
calf	a young elephant
drought	a period of time during which there is little or no rain
habitat	the natural environment where an animal or plant lives
herbivore	an animal that eats only plants
incisor	a kind of tooth. An elephant's tusks are very, very long incisors

ivory	a smooth, hard white substance that forms the tusks of elephants and other animals
mammal	an animal with a backbone and hair on its body that drinks milk from its mother when it is born
matriarch	female leader of a group
pachyderm	another word for elephant. It comes from the Greek word for 'thick-skinned'.

predator	an animal that hunts and eats other animals to survive	species	a group of plants or animals that are the same in many ways
proboscidea	ancient relatives of elephants that included mastodons and mammoths	trunk	the long, flexible nose of an elephant
savannah	a flat grassland area with scattered trees in a hot region of the world	tusk	a very long, pointed tooth that sticks far out from the side of an animal's mouth, usually one of a pair
sea cow	a modern relative of the elephant that lives in the ocean. Also called a manatee.	visible	able to be seen

INDEX

A

African elephants **16, 17, 18, 21, 25, 41**

Asian elephants **17, 18, 21, 25, 36, 40**

B

baby elephants **13, 30, 35, 36, 37**

bathing **10, 30, 31**

C

communication **10, 13, 19, 35, 36, 45**

cooling **10, 25, 30, 31, 42**

D

danger **43**

digging **29, 30**

drinking **19, 30**

E

ears **16, 17, 25**

eating **18, 28, 29, 36**

F

feet **22, 41**

female elephants **35, 37**

food **29, 36**

G

giraffes **10**

group behaviour **9, 10, 29, 35, 36**

H

habitats **41, 42, 43**

hair **13**

herbivores **29**

herds **9, 35**

hyraxes **41**

I

ivory **21, 43**

L

life span **41**

M

male elephants **29, 35**

mammals **13, 41**

mammoths **41**

manatee **41**

mastodons **41**

matriarch **35**

memory **9**

mother elephants **9, 13, 36-37**

mud **10, 25, 31**

muscles **18**

N

nose **18**

P

pachyderm **25**

playing **10, 30, 31, 36**

S

safety **35, 36**

size **10, 16, 17, 40**

skin **22, 24, 25, 31**

sleep **29, 35**

smell **18**

sounds **10, 35, 36**

speed **23**

swimming **30**

T

tail **13**

teeth **21, 29**

tigers **43**

trunk **17-19, 30, 35-36**

tusks **17, 21, 29-30, 35, 41, 43**

W

walking **22, 23**

water **18, 30**

weight **30, 40**

CREDITS

Elephants is an *All About Animals* fact book
published by Reader's Digest Young Families, Inc.

Written by Sarah Albee

Copyright © 2006 Reader's Digest Young Families, Inc.
This edition was adapted and published in 2008 by
The Reader's Digest Association Limited

11 Westferry Circus, Canary Wharf, London E14 4HE
® Reader's Digest, the Pegasus logo and Reader's Digest Young Families
are registered trademarks of
The Reader's Digest Association, Inc.

We are committed to both the quality of our products and the service we provide to our customers.
We value your comments, so please feel free to contact us on
08705 113366 or via our website at: www.readersdigest.co.uk
If you have any comments or suggestions about the content of our books,
you can contact us at: gbeditorial@readersdigest.co.uk

Printed in China

Reader's Digest®
YOUNG FAMILIES

Book code: 640-007 UP0000-1
ISBN: 978 0 276 44324 4